Phyllis Webstad

As founder of Orange Shirt Day and ambassador for Orange Shirt Society, Phyllis Webstad facilitates dialogue around the Indian Residential School system and creates space for healing. When Phyllis was just six-years-old, she was forced to attend Residential School. Upon arrival, her brand-new orange shirt that was gifted to her by her granny was taken away and never returned. That cruel action resulted in Phyllis feeling unimportant and as if she did not matter. The colour orange has become a symbol of the effects of Indian Residential Schools and a physical symbol for 'Every Child Matters'. Over Phyllis's career she has acquired diplomas in both Business Administration from Nicola Valley Institute of Technology and Accounting from Thompson Rivers University (TRU). A published author, Phyllis has several books that share her story in her own words. Phyllis is Northern Secwépemc (Shuswap) from the Stswecem'c Xgat'tem First Nation (Canoe Creek Indian Band), and she currently resides in Williams Lake, British Columbia with her husband.

Emily Kewageshig

Emily Kewageshig is an Anishnaabe artist and visual storyteller from Saugeen First Nation No. 29. Her work captures the interconnection of life forms using both traditional and contemporary materials and methods. Her work is centered around themes of birth, death, and rebirth as they are closely intertwined in both her cultural teachings and personal lived experiences. Emily attended Sheridan College's Visual and Creative Arts program, as well as OCAD University's Indigenous Visual Culture program. She continues to create artwork for various organizations to highlight Indigenous knowledge and culture.

Orange Shirt Day

Since 2013, each year on September 30th, we wear orange to honour Residential School Survivors like Phyllis. We honour their experiences and the experiences of their families. Orange Shirt Day is an opportunity for Indigenous peoples, local governments, schools and communities to come together in the spirit of reconciliation and hope for future generations of children. It is a day to reaffirm that Every Child Matters.

Canada Based Toll-Free Help Lines

24-hour National Indian Residential School crisis line — 1-866-925-4419
First Nations and Inuit Mental Health and Wellness — 1-855-242-3310
Kids Help Phone — 1-800-668-6868
Suicide Prevention and Support — 1-833-456-4566
9-1-1 Emergency

Territory Acknowledgements

Phyllis Webstad and Medicine Wheel Publishing acknowledge that this book was created on the traditional territories of the Coast Salish people including the Sc'ianew people, the Lekwungen people, the T'Sou-ke people as well as the traditional territories of the Interior Salish people, the Secwépemc (Shuswap) including the T'exelcemc First Nation (Williams Lake Indian Band) and the Xatśūll First Nation (Soda Creek Indian Band).

With Our Orange Hearts

EVERY CHILD MATTERS

Phyllis Webstad   Emily Kewageshig

Orange Shirt Day
is a special day.
Wear one,
and unite today!

I, Phyllis,
shared my story true,
about my orange shirt
that once was new.

My orange shirt
was taken away
at a lonely place
where I had to stay.

This made me cry
and feel very sad.
Missing my family
and the orange shirt I had.

Sharing my orange shirt story
and how it made me feel
helped me to know
that I could heal.

My feelings matter
just like yours do.
Share your orange shirt story
about your feelings, too.

Today we wear orange
to honour and be
together as one
human family.

I have hope for true
reconciliation,
help spread orange
from nation to nation.

Every Child Matters
including you and me.
With our orange hearts,
we walk in harmony.

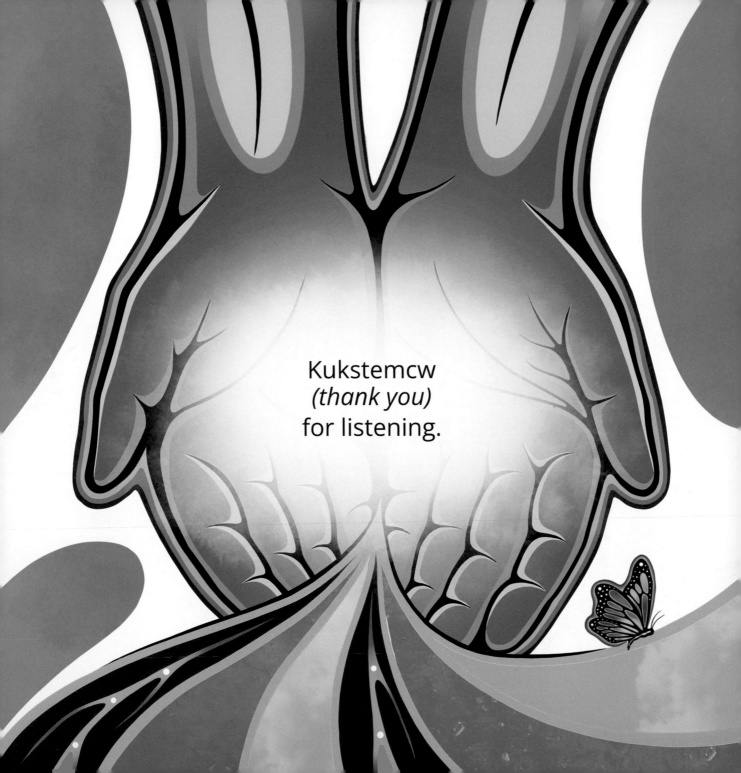

Kukstemcw
(thank you)
for listening.

EVERY CHILD MATTERS

More Books at:
www.medicinewheelpublishing.com

Medicine Wheel Publishing

Funded by the Government of Canada

Financé par le gouvernement du Canada

Canada